DESIGN
the
LIFE
YOU
LOVE

DESIGN the LIFE YOU LOVE*

no prior creative experience necessary!

my life

by ayse birsel

a step-by-step guide
to building a meaningful future

TEN SPEED PRESS
BERKELEY

CONTENTS

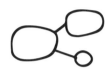

03. RECONSTRUCTION

04. EXPRESSION

= unique

LIVING THE LIFE

THE END IS ONLY THE BEGINNING!

welcome to designing your life!

happy

All design involves risk and daring. After all, you are creating something new and original. If you are here, you are courageous!

Dear reader,

YOU ARE COURAGEOUS!

If you are reading this book, it means that you want to be the designer of your own life; that you are interested in thinking about your life proactively; that you have things to explore and changes you want to make creatively.

This book is for anyone who, like me, thinks that your life is your most important project. It does not require that you have any design or creative experience, just the desire to explore your life from a new point of view and to learn to think like a designer.

Welcome to designing the life you love.

ABOUT DESIGN THE LIFE YOU LOVE

Design the Life You Love started as an experiment. I had just finished putting my creative process on paper, as a tool to share with my team at Birsel + Seck, the design studio I lead with my husband, Bibi Seck, in New York, and our clients. But first I needed a test project. What better testing ground than my own life, something I have come to consider my biggest project? I first shared it with my friends, who've helped me to fine-tune the steps and given me the confidence to go do it. Then I did my first workshop. And things started to grow from there. Which brings us to this book you're holding in your hands!

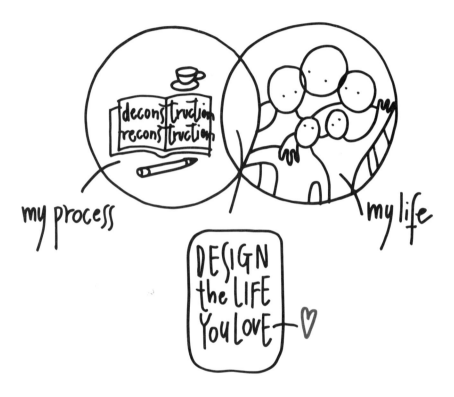

my process

my life

DESIGN
the LIFE
You LOVE

Design the Life You Love is the intersection of my design process,
Deconstruction:Reconstruction, and my biggest project, my life.

STORY of DESIGN the LIFE YOU LOVE

YOUR STRATEGIC INTENT IN LIFE...

ONE DAY, I WAS AT A MEETING WHERE WE WERE ASKED TO SUM UP OUR STRATEGIC INTENT IN ONE SENTENCE.

my strategic intent is to design the life I love!*

* BEING THE ONLY DESIGNER IN THE ROOM, I WANTED TO SAY SOMETHING ABOUT DESIGN + BE WITTY. LITTLE DID I KNOW THE IMPORTANCE THIS WOULD HAVE FOR ME!

SOON AFTER, I MET BIBI. AND MY LIFE STARTED TO DESIGN ITSELF.

... PRODUCTS, PARTNERSHIP, CHILDREN, HOME, OFFICE.

THEN THE RECESSION HIT.
WE FOUND OURSELVES WITH A
LOT OF TIME ON OUR HANDS.

LEAH SUGGESTED I USE THIS TIME TO ARTICULATE
HOW I THINK AS A DESIGNER. AND I DID!

I CALLED MY PROCESS DECONSTRUCTION · RECONSTRUCTION.

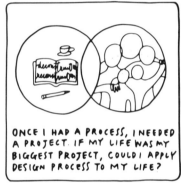

ONCE I HAD A PROCESS, I NEEDED
A PROJECT. IF MY LIFE WAS MY
BIGGEST PROJECT, COULD I APPLY
DESIGN PROCESS TO MY LIFE?

MY FIRST WORKSHOP WAS IN 2010. I WASN'T ALONE. MANY PEOPLE WANTED
TO DESIGN THEIR LIVES CREATIVELY, OPTIMISTICALLY. LIKE YOU!

As I was starting Design the Life You Love, I received this message from my friend and mentor, Ralph Caplan, author of *By Design*.

"Dear Ayse,
When it comes to life,
there is no such
thing as design.
There is only redesign."

Ralph has been a big influence in my life since the day I met him when I was 24 years old, and his words rang so true to me. Indeed, you will be redesigning your life. Except this time you will have a design process and tools to do it.

RALPH CAPLAN

WHAT IS THIS BOOK?

This is a workbook to use interactively, take notes on, paste pictures into, draw on its pages, color in if you feel in the mood . . . then refer back to each time you have a problem you want to solve or just want to refresh yourself on the process of designing your life.

This is an evolving process, one that you get better at the more you do it, and that you can adapt to the changes in your life with its ups and downs.

But I shouldn't really call it a workbook. This is actually a PLAYBOOK. A book in which to think playfully!

This little rabbit will remind you throughout this book: Be Playful! Playful is the mood of design, because when you're playing, you don't worry about making mistakes or failing. Just like when you were a child.

HOW TO USE THIS BOOK

20 Minutes
Do 20 minutes or so
and then take a break.
Come back later or
the next day.

Always Right
There are no wrong
answers here, only
your answers.

drawing + text

playful

Draw and Write
You don't have to
draw like Picasso,
but just draw.

Playful
Play when you're
designing in this book.
Like a child. Don't forget
that this rabbit will be
your reminder!

WHY DESIGN?

Design is about identifying and working within given constraints to arrive at new and better solutions. Life, just like a design problem, is full of constraints: time, money, age, location, circumstances, etc. You cannot have everything. If you want more, you have to be creative about how to make what you need and what you want coexist. This requires design thinking.

Often what we want and what we need oppose each other (i.e., you want to go on vacation but you need to make money...). Creativity is making the two coexist (like figuring out how to make money while on vacation).

THINKING LIKE A DESIGNER

Here is how to think like a designer:

- think positively;

- put yourself in the shoes of other people and see things from their perspective;

- see the big picture;

- collaborate with others, as this makes the ideas so much richer;

- and last but not least, always ask yourself "what if?" and take your answers seriously.

As you design your life, remember to think holistically and collaboratively, like a designer, with optimism and empathy. And remember to ask yourself, what if I did this?

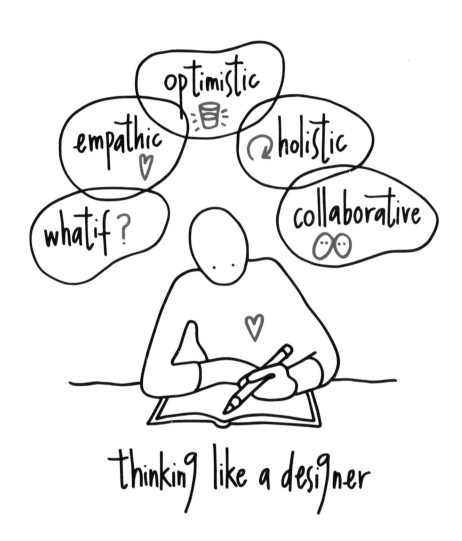

thinking like a designer

MY PROCESS

In this book I will share how to apply my design process, Deconstruction:Reconstruction, to your life in four simple steps.

01.
DECONSTRUCTION

Taking the whole apart.

02.
POINT OF VIEW

Seeing it differently.

03.
RECONSTRUCTION

Putting it back together.

04.
EXPRESSION

Giving it form.

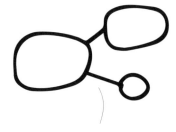 = *unique*

Deconstructing and breaking current reality is necessary
to enable us to shift our perspective—to see the same things
differently—in order to reconstruct a new reality that is
more than the sum of its parts.

FROM PRODUCT DESIGN

My process comes from product design. Everything we use in everyday life is designed by a designer. I've designed furniture, office systems, kitchen utensils, pots and pans...even a toilet seat, using Deconstruction:Reconstruction. The following are some of my favorite examples from our work at Birsel + Seck, and what I learned from them.

Zoe Washlet

Teneo Storage System

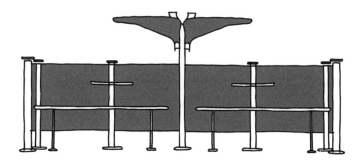

Resolve Office System

Madame Dakar Lounge Chair

TOILETS AS SEATS

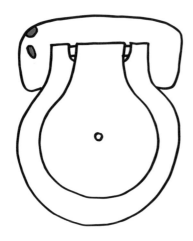

One of my first deconstructions was a toilet seat, of all things! It was as simple as breaking "toilet seat" into "toilet" and "seat." That is all it took for me to realize that a toilet seat is a SEAT. It is for sitting, and as such, it should be designed to be COMFORTABLE.

This was the starting point of designing the Zoe Washlet for the sanitary company TOTO; it was unofficially dubbed the world's most comfortable toilet seat.

take away!

Deconstructing even very familiar things helps us break our preconceptions, so we can see the same things from a whole new perspective. As a designer of products, or of life for that matter, your role is to not take what came before you for granted. Why be limited by someone else's idea of doing things when you can come up with a much better solution?

OFFICES + POINTS

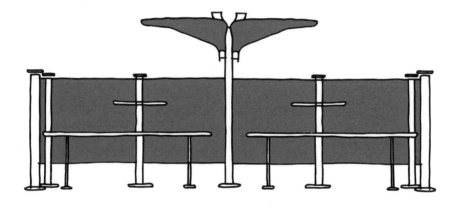

Design is turning a constraint into an opportunity. With
Resolve, an office system I designed for Herman Miller,
the constraint was size. Smaller and smaller cubicles
were turning offices into Dilbert-land. Going along with
the constraint instead of opposing it, we shrank the
cubicle to its smallest possible footprint and imagined
it as a point in space. This became the start of a new
idea, an office system based on poles in 120-degree
configurations instead of the traditional office panels.

take away!

Turning a constraint into an
opportunity can help us think outside
the box, no pun intended. Think now of
a constraint you have in your own life.
Can you see it as an advantage?
This shift in our point of view will be
at the center of our creative process.

STORAGE AS BODY

When Bibi and I were working on the Teneo Storage System, we realized that if it weren't for storage our stuff would be sitting on the floor in piles. You need structure to hold stuff upright, kind of like a skeleton holding up a body. This led us to think about storage not as a box but as a body: structure as skeleton; organs as the storage units (drawers, shelves, etc.); and skin as the cladding, or covering materials (metal, wood, felt, etc.).

Thinking through the lens of a metaphor helped us reimagine storage.

take away!

Thinking about your life through metaphors is one of the most powerful tools in your toolbox, as you will see. We will use metaphors to shift our perspective from our life today to our life tomorrow. (This is coming up on page 116, if you want to take a quick peek.)

SEATING + AFRICA

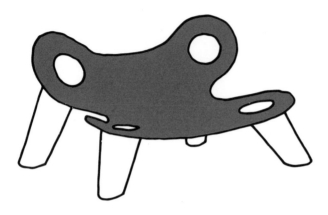

When Patrizia Moroso, head of the amazing Italian
furniture company Moroso, asked us to work on the
M'Afrique project to showcase the design power of Africa,
we were ecstatic. I found my inspiration in the women
of Dakar. Incredibly tall and broad, and robed in the most
beautiful colors, fabrics, and shapes, they look like walking
sculptures. I captured their essence in Madame Dakar, a
gorgeous, oversized lounge chair. This project is very close
to my heart, a carte blanche to do what I want, with
little compromise.

take away!

Design can also be fun, personal, and very close to your heart. Your life is your design. Make it resemble you, reflect you, and be close to your heart.

OK, TIME TO GET STARTED

All you need is:

- Your book

- Favorite pen or pencil

- Optimism and playfulness

- A cup of coffee or tea

- A comfortable place at home or in a cafe

- Some music if you'd like

- 20 minutes at a time

Shall we?

A cup of tea symbolizes "getting started" to me. It's my creative habit.
(For more on this, see *The Creative Habit* by Twyla Tharp, from the reading
list on page 250.) What is yours?

WHAT WILL WE DO TOGETHER?

1. Warm up the right brain

2. Deconstruct your life

warm-up

deconstruct

3. Look for inspiration

4. Shift your POV from the present...

inspiration

today

5. ...to the future

tomorrow

6. Reconstruct life and
decide what really matters

choice

7. Express the life you love
as a great new design

design

8. Live the life you love

living

 = unique

00. WARM UP

LET'S WARM UP
Tool #1

I start every project by drawing. I learned this when I was in design school. It's like a little signal to the right brain saying, wake up!

For those of you who don't think of yourselves as "creative," don't worry. No one is grading you...

So, pick something to draw. Draw your cat or dog, or yourself in the mirror, or your coffee cup, or your kid (this is a hard one: see next page), or your partner/friend (this will get you laughs). If you're not at home, draw someone sitting across from you on the subway, or in the cafe or library.

Just draw!

I drew my daughters. It is not easy to catch your children in one position for a long time, unless they're playing on their phones or watching TV!

Draw someone or something.

⏱ Timing: about 5 minutes

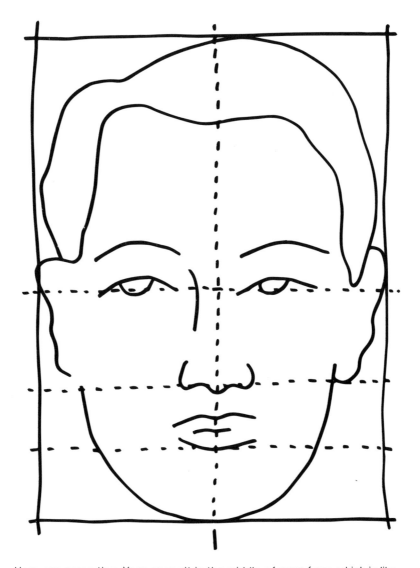

Here are some tips: Your eyes sit in the middle of your face, which is like a rectangle. Tip of your nose is in the middle of your eyes and chin. Your mouth is in the middle of the space between the tip of your nose and chin. Try it and you will see.

Draw something every time you come back to this book.

🕐 Timing: 5 minutes

...reminder:
don't judge, just play

Draw something else another day. Turn to page 220 when you run out of space here. And keep at it and warm-up your right brain, just like you would with your body before exercising. Use a sketchbook when you run out of space in this book.

LET'S DESIGN LIFE...

Now that you're warmed up.

STEP 1   Deconstruct your life.

STEP 2   Form a POV of your life.

STEP 3   Reconstruct your life.

STEP 4   Express your life as a new design.

How does this work? You can jump to page 62 to start designing your life right away or deconstruct and reconstruct soup first as an example!

...OR SOUP!

Imagine for a second that you're making a soup.

STEP 1 is deciding what kind of soup and listing the ingredients. That list of ingredients is Deconstruction.

STEP 2 is thinking about the ingredients. Maybe you want to change them because you're inspired by a new recipe, or because you like to improvise, or because you're limited by what you have in your pantry? This is forming a POV.

STEP 3 is making choices. Like deciding to try a new recipe but improvising on it based on what you have in the pantry. Putting it together in your own new way is Reconstruction.

STEP 4 is making it real. Cooking your version of the soup, serving it in a nice bowl, sharing it with family on a cold winter night—in short, creating a great experience. That experience is Expression.

You want to give it a try?

STEP 1: DECONSTRUCTION

Let's try designing a new Chicken Noodle Soup!

This is what Chicken Noodle Soup
looks like before we deconstruct it.

This is what Chicken Noodle Soup looks like once we
deconstruct it.

What I like so much about deconstruction is that looking
at the parts, I feel that I have complete freedom to
change them. I can keep some; bring in new ingredients,
processes, and utensils, and delete some others. Shall we?

STEP 2: POV

What is your opinion of Chicken Noodle Soup? Too traditional? More of a flu remedy? Not vegetarian? Not practical to eat on the go? Well, let's change some things and see if we like it better.

What if... we switch chicken to tofu, take out the noodles, add in kale and cayenne pepper for a little kick...and perhaps we puree it. And who said soup has to be hot? What if we freeze it? But hold on; how are we going to eat that? What if we put it on a stick, like an ice-cream pop? We'd have a soup pop.

This organic process of shifting from what we know, Chicken Noodle Soup, to what we can imagine, the soup pop, is the heart of our creativity.

SOUP POP

STEP 3: RECONSTRUCTION

Shifting our perspective on soup helped us reconstruct
a new kind of soup.

When we changed chicken to tofu,
we shifted to a vegetarian soup.

chicken ↝ tofu

Shifting from hot to frozen, we
challenged our traditional notion
of soup (and why not?).

hot ↝ frozen

Freezing the soup allowed us to serve
it on a stick. And if you can serve it on
a stick, you can now eat it anywhere.

bowl ↝ on a stick

Our reconstruction is a cold soup that
merges two familiar ideas, soup and
Popsicle, to create a new idea, soup pop
that you can conveniently eat anywhere.
So how shall we express this idea?

table ↝ anywhere

STEP 4: EXPRESSION

NEW SOUP!

CHICKEN
Soup

SPACE
Soup

What if we expressed it as Space Food, a soup you can eat in a space station in outer space? Easy to store for long periods of time, no drip, no fuss, no bowls, and nutritious, too.

That was easy! If you want to try it, pick a soup of your choice, follow the steps of the Chicken Noodle Soup, and reinvent your own soup!

Or your life.

DESIGNING A LIFE USING DE:RE IS LIKE MAKING SOUP

Chicken soup, or life for that matter, is not an unbreakable whole but a combination of parts and processes we can question, manipulate, and change. And every time we do, we create something new.

Keep the soup example in mind as you design your life. And let's get started!

if life is soup:

what are the ingredients?

which ingredients
do you want to change, replace, keep?

what if you change
the way you've always made it?

what if you change
the way you eat it?

let's start!

In designing your life, the end user is you! Use this workbook to think about yourself and your life–unabashedly, for once.

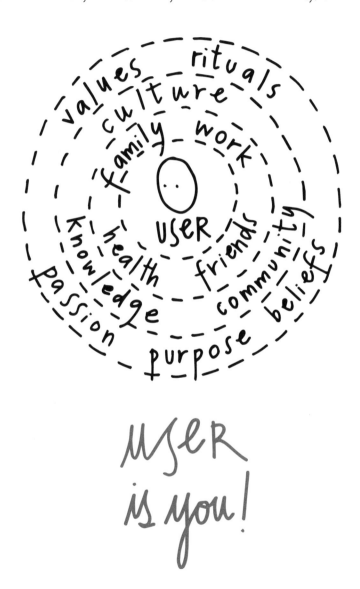

USER
is you!

= unique

Deconstruction
*

01. DECONSTRUCTION

"Divide each difficulty into as many parts as is feasible and necessary to resolve it."

Deconstruction is not a new idea, as demonstrated by this Descartes quote, but a very powerful one for tackling big subjects, especially one as vast as our life!

RENÉ DESCARTES

DECONSTRUCTION
Step #1

Deconstruction, our first step, is about breaking something into its building blocks to understand what it is made up of without the connections and links that inadvertently form our preconceptions. It renders complexity simple by breaking it into smaller, more manageable parts.

However, once you break something apart, you won't be able to put it back together the way it was before.

So here is my disclaimer: if you have the perfect life, close this book now. Because once you deconstruct your life, you won't be able to put it back together in quite the same way. Turn the page to see what I mean!

LIFE DECONSTRUCTED

What I love about Deconstruction is that there is no right or wrong way to do it. It is all good.

Some of my favorite examples of deconstruction are exploded views of cameras, like the one I drew here.

What do you think? Can you put it back together again just like it was before? I think not! (Unless you're a specialist of cameras.) Same thing with your life.

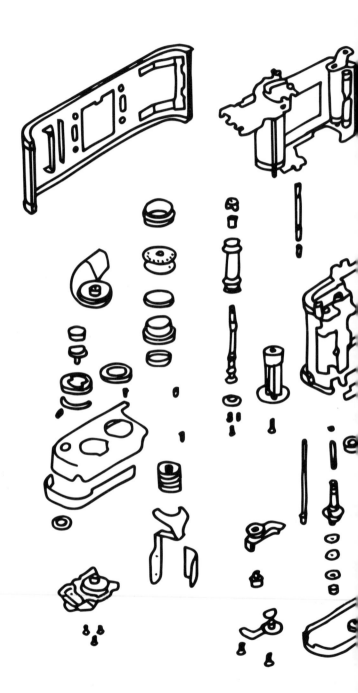

REMINDER!

You know that game where someone says "apple" and you say the first thing that comes to your mind (green, red, Steve Jobs, New York, pie...) and there are no wrong answers? It is the same thing here. Go with whatever comes to your mind naturally, and don't judge your answers.

Design process is all about thinking by doing.

And doing by playing.

There are no right or wrong answers.

Especially because some of the best solutions come from the worst initial ideas.

playful!

Another way of saying "playful" is "no judgment." The rabbit will remind you to play.

LET'S DECONSTRUCT!
Tool #2

Let's deconstruct your life into its building blocks. Remember
how we did this with chicken soup? We wrote out the
ingredients... Same thing with your life, except there may
be a few more ingredients in your life.

When you're ready, turn the page to get started on your
deconstruction map.

chicken   onions   carrots   salt+pepper

water   herbs   celery   noodles

fire   pot   bowl   spoon

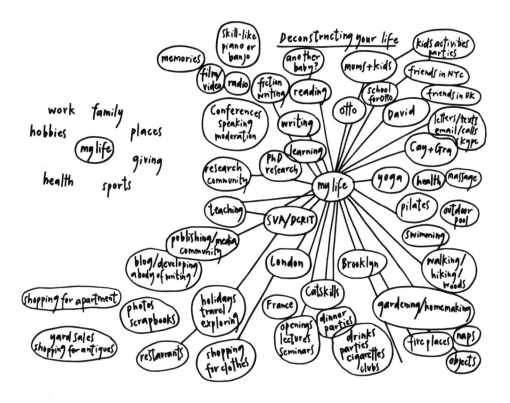

Deconstructing your life

work   family
hobbies   places
      my life
            giving
health   sports

my life

- Skill-like piano or banjo
- memories
- film/video
- radio
- fiction writing
- reading
- another baby?
- mums+kids
- school for otto
- kids activities parties
- friends in NYC
- friends in UK
- Conferences speaking moderation
- writing
- otto
- David
- letters/texts email/calls
- skype
- learning
- Cay+Gra
- PhD research
- research community
- yoga
- health
- massage
- teaching
- pilates
- outdoor pool
- SVA/DCRIT
- swimming
- publishing/media community
- London
- Brooklyn
- walking/hiking/woods
- blog/developing a body of writing
- shopping for apartment
- photos scrapbooks
- holidays travel/exploring
- Catskills
- France
- gardening/homemaking
- yard sales shopping for antiques
- restaurants
- shopping for clothes
- openings lectures seminars
- dinner parties
- drinks parties cigarettes clubs
- fire places
- naps
- objects

Here is a deconstruction map from Alice Twemlow, author and chair of the Design Criticism Department at the School of Visual Arts (SVA). She first noted the main building blocks on the left and then mapped out her life freely.

I filled in the first building blocks for you. Add on and fill in the page until you run out of thoughts.

⏱ Timing: about 10 minutes.

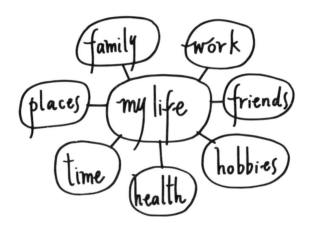

Use this page to note anything that comes to your mind as you deconstruct.

Here is another way of thinking about it. Fill the whole page and spill over to the next.

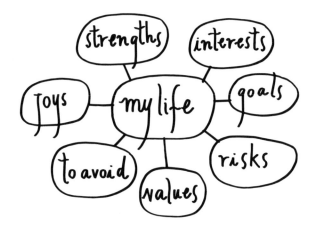

Here is one you can totally customize.

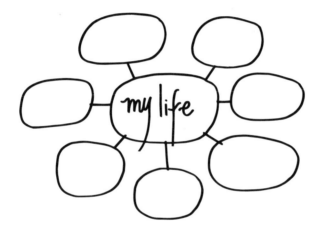

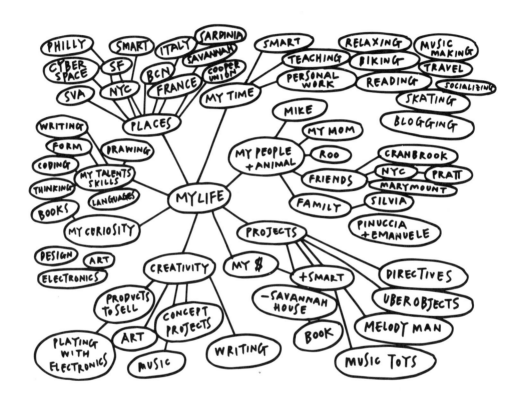

Here is a deconstruction map from Carla Diana, a humanistic designer of robots. I love how she customized her building blocks, like "my curiosity," "my talents and skills," and "my $." You can make up your own building blocks.

If you need two pages, go for it!

Now, take just one aspect of your life and deconstruct it.

⏱ Timing: about 5 minutes.

my life

I deconstructed "time" as an exercise and included everything I could think about time in it: my day (twice), my age, and my past, present, and future, and everything that it made me think of.

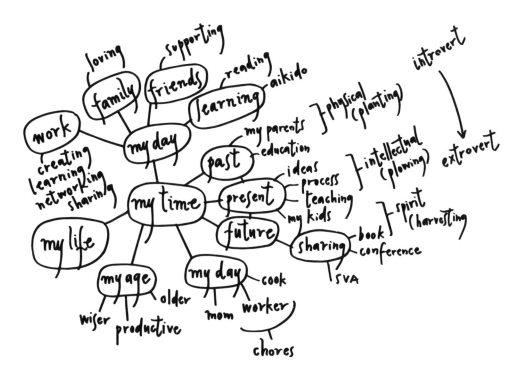

Thinking about my past, present, and future led me to my life metaphor, a tree, which is why there are references to planting, plowing, and harvesting on the right side of my chart. More on this on page 126.

DE: FOUR QUADRANTS
Tool #3

Now that you've become a master of deconstruction, let's do my favorite version, the four quadrants.

Deconstruct your life into four quadrants:

- Emotion

- Physical

- Intellect

- Spirit

See how your life balances out, or doesn't. This is like doing a 360 on your life.

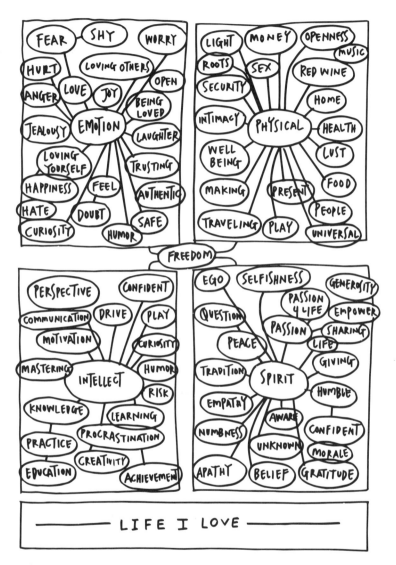

LIFE I LOVE

I used Lee Iley's quadrants here as inspiration. Lee is a New York-based graphic designer and one of my cool collaborators. Note how freedom belongs in all quadrants: I feel free, I am free, I am a free thinker, and I am a free spirit!

Put one entry in each quadrant, i.e.

- Emotion: love my cat
- Physical: small apartment
- Intellect: learning one new thing/day
- Spirit: helping in the soup kitchen

Do it once, putting one thing in each quadrant. Do a second round, a third, a fourth, etc., until you run out of things to add. Use your first deconstruction maps to remind you of stuff.

Some things will want to go in two or more quadrants. Just put them in the first one that comes to your mind, or note that they belong in more than one place. See Lee's example on the preceding page, with "freedom" belonging in all four.

Some quadrants may be easier to fill than others. And that is the whole point. See how yours balances out. You will be able to come back and add as you go through the book.

🕐 Timing: about 10 minutes.

emotion ♡

physical 〰

This is about what
you feel. It goes through
your heart.

This is about what
you can measure. It relates
to your body.

This is about what
you think. It occupies
your mind.

This is about what
you believe. It is from
your soul.

intellect @

spirit ☺

emotion of the life l love ♡

- -

intellect of the life l love ☺

physical of the life I love ♏

- -

spirit of the life I love ☯

emotion of the life I love ♡

- -

intellect of the life I love @

physical of the life I love ༃

- -

spirit of the life I love Ⓢ

Let's do a short recap.

insights AHA!

Write one insight or AHA! moment you had as you deconstructed your life using the four quadrants.

too little/too much

One thing that you have too much or too little of...

opportunity ✚

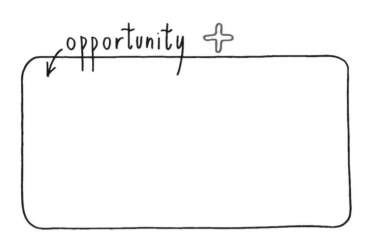

If you could note one opportunity...

constraints ━

How about one constraint...

 = unique

Point of View
*

02. POINT OF VIEW

Now that we've deconstructed our life, let's think about it from different points of view. Everything depends on how we look at it!

WILLIAM SHAKESPEARE

"There is nothing either good or bad, but thinking makes it so."

POINT OF VIEW
STEP #2

Our point of view informs how we think about something.
So, what if we can look at the same old things in life but see
them differently? This ability to shift our POV intentionally
is at the heart of our creativity.

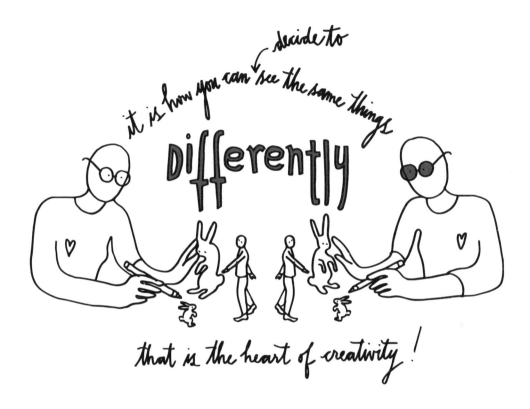

it is how you can decide to see the same things

Differently

that is the heart of creativity!

Seeing differently is like putting on an imaginary pair of special glasses and filtering the information through them. Your life is what it is. What is different is what glasses you choose to decide how you want to see the same things differently.

DESIGN + CHOICES

As you deconstructed your life, I am sure you came across things you wished weren't there. We all have them—vices, conflicts, weaknesses. And that is the point of designing our life—to keep what we love, get rid of what we don't want, and transform what we cannot change to something we can utilize to create a more positive outcome.

But let's first look at how some of the best design thinkers see things differently, creatively, to create new ideas.

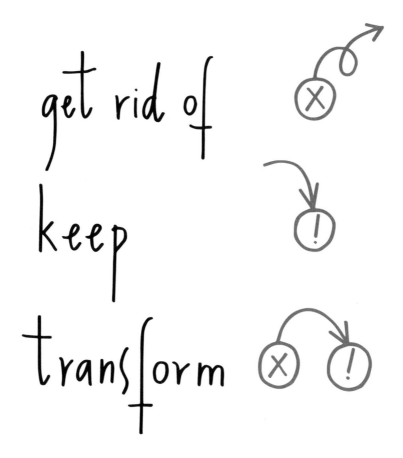

get rid of

keep

transform

Identifying what to keep, what to get rid of, what new connections to make, and what to transform to our advantage is a huge step forward in our design process.

EXAMPLES OF THINKING DIFFERENTLY

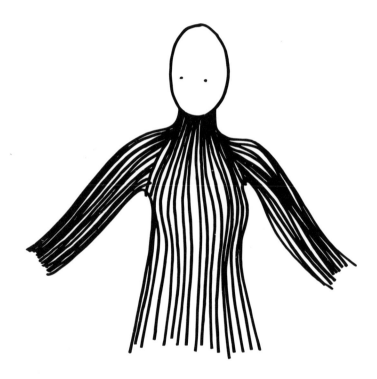

When Japanese fashion designer Issey Miyake created a new travel collection, he took wrinkles—a nuisance and a constraint of traveling—and translated them into the fabric with specially designed permanent pleats. His innovative PLEATS PLEASE Collection requires no ironing, folds beautifully, and molds to your body when worn. He made constraints his opportunity.

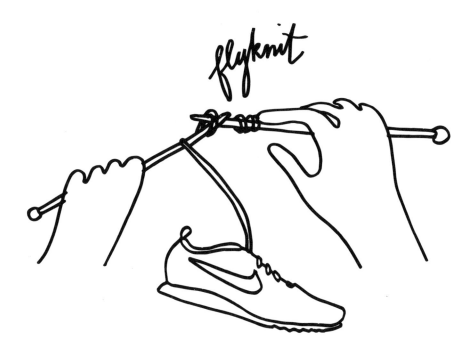

flyknit

When the designers at Nike decided to create a shoe that would eliminate all fabric waste, they turned to knitting—a centuries-old tradition—and created the amazing Flyknit, a knit shoe. Old ideas applied in a new context can be an incredible resource for innovation.

Sam Farber watched his wife struggle to peel potatoes due to arthritis and he felt her pain. From that empathy, the now legendary OXO Good Grips were born. The soft-grip design is a feature that we take for granted today. Putting yourself in someone else's shoes is not only compassionate but often the first step in solving problems.

RICE COOKER

Steve Jobs explained that the idea for the magnetic power connector on Apple laptops came from the design of Japanese rice cookers. The problem was the same: you don't want your rice cooker or your laptop to fall on the floor if someone trips on the power cord. Taking a good idea out of one context and applying it in a totally new context can be a very powerful tool to help you see things differently.

HEROES AS INSPIRATION

Our first POV tool to help us think differently and shift
our point of view is the inspiration our heroes provide.

We are inspired by people—heroes, real and fictional—people
we know personally or not at all. These heroes tell us
something about our values, beliefs, and the kind of life
we aspire to live.

my hero

Who are your heroes? What do they tell you about the life you want to design?

EXAMPLES OF HEROES

Rowena Reed Kostellow (1900–1988) is my hero. She was a woman ahead of her time who created a whole new methodology of design in three dimensions; she was a great educator who formed generations of designers, and was known for her generosity, strength, and kindness.

You've got to check out John Waters's heroes from his book, *Role Models*: singer Johnny Mathis, writer Tennessee Williams, a gay reality-porn auteur, a lesbian stripper called Lady Zorro, and atheist leader Madalyn Murray O'Hair!

Hani Hong, an out-of-the-box-thinking marketing director, cited her mom as her hero, seen here in their family passport photo in 1975, a few days before she escaped Vietnam with her five children. Her husband was able to join them a few months later. Hani explains, "My mother was thirty-four. I love how courageous she looks here, knowing of our pending escape and with five young children. The secret is unconditional love!"

PAULA SCHER

"That's easy! Tina Fey for being brilliantly funny, creative, and successful, while not taking herself too seriously. Anna Wintour for her steely commitment to excellence. Paula Scher for her feisty, opinionated, obsessive artistry. Julie Taymor. Cleopatra. Nora Ephron. See a theme here?" says Linda Tischler, senior design editor of *Fast Company*.

YOUR HEROES
Tool #4

Now it's your turn!

Who are your heroes? Write their names and list the qualities that endear them to you.

Don't forget to draw a little icon or a symbol for each hero.

ZAHA

ZAHA'S MOLE
- PERSEVERANCE
- P.O.V.
- STRENGTH

RODRIGUEZ

RODRIGUEZ'S GUITAR
- HUMILITY
- COMMUNICATION
- DEPTH

TIBOR KALMAN

COLORS MAGAZINE
- WORLD VIEW
- FIRST DESIGNER I KNEW
- HUMOR

MICHAEL JACKSON

THE GLOVE
- SEXUALITY
- EXPLAINING
- DEFINING
- CHALLENGING

Michael Robinson is a wonderful designer. I love the icons he created for his heroes, especially Zaha Hadid's mole and Michael Jackson's glove!

Fill in with your heroes. And don't forget to list their qualities.

🕐 Timing: about 10 minutes.

my hero: _____
_____
_____
_____
_____

icon/symbol

my hero: _____
_____
_____
_____
_____

icon/symbol

my hero: _____
_____
_____
_____
_____

icon/symbol

my hero: _____
_____
_____
_____
_____

icon/symbol

CROSS OUT THE HERO

Now that you listed your heroes...
CROSS OUT THEIR NAMES and put yours!

Their qualities are your qualities. The values you recognize
and admire in your heroes are your values.

As Sue Knight, the great NLP (neuro-linguistic programming)
teacher and author, tells her students, me among them,
"If someone can do it—anyone can do it."

Keep your values at the top of your mind as you continue
to design your life.

PUT YOUR OWN NAME HERE!

Many things can change in life but our values are a constant. They are the foundation of our life design.

"Human thinking depends on metaphor. We understand new or complex things in relation to things we already know."

When you're designing a life, you shift from what you know to what you can imagine. You're defining an idea you have an inkling for but that you can't quite put your finger on. This moment of creative transition is ideal for metaphors.

JONATHAN HAIDT

METAPHORS

Metaphors are my favorite creative tool!

Metaphors take your mind on a magical detour, seemingly away from your subject, while actually sending you deep into the heart of the matter. They provide hooks to explore details otherwise forgotten. They make complexity manageable. The shifting from present to future metaphors that we will do allows us to compare our baseline to our future vision for our life.

Here are a few metaphors to help get you going. Your metaphor for today and tomorrow can be the same, like my tree metaphor; a version of each other, like a dinner today and a feast tomorrow; or two very different ones, like a circus today and a lake tomorrow.

I learned about metaphors from my friend and collaborator Jim Long, director of research at Herman Miller. Jim had done a study where he asked people to describe their organizations through metaphors. Beehive, circus, theater, emergency room, and zoo...

bee hive circus the

What is key here is not only the metaphor but its description. A beehive could be the best of organizations, very organized, productive, with a sweet product. But it could also be the worst place for creativity, individualism, and initiative taking, with everyone working as drones under a queen bee.

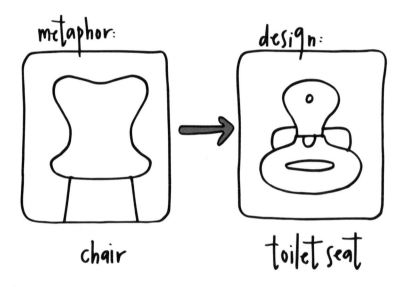

metaphor:

chair

design:

toilet seat

The metaphor for the Zoe Washlet that I designed for TOTO (page 28) was a chair, albeit one with a hole in it. This was a fundamental shift in perspective that helped us make a radically comfortable toilet seat.

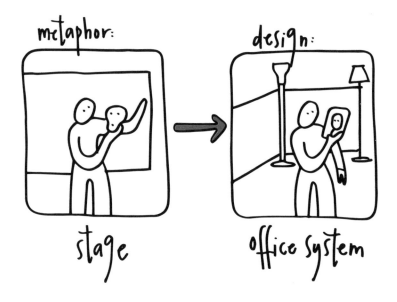

metaphor:

stage

design:

office system

The metaphor for the Resolve Office System we designed for Herman Miller (page 30) was a theater stage for the performance of work, designed to be lightweight and easy to change and adapt to different performances. Here the performers are the people at work.

"Whenever I have trouble writing, I think about the pace of baseball. It's slow. You strike out a lot, even if you're great. It's mostly individual, but when you have to work together, it must be perfect. My desktop picture is of the Red Sox during the World Series. They aren't winning; they're just grinding out another play. This, for me, is very helpful to have in my mind while writing."

I came across Greta Gerwig's use of baseball as a metaphor for writing in the *New York Times* Sunday Magazine. What she does with writing, we will do for our life.

GRETA GERWIG

LET'S USE A METAPHOR
TO THINK ABOUT THE PRESENT

Can you think of a metaphor for your life today?
This will serve as your baseline for your current life.

my life is a beehive

LET'S USE A METAPHOR
TO THINK ABOUT THE FUTURE

Can you think of a metaphor for your life tomorrow?
This will serve as your vision for your future life.

my life will be a flying machine

EXAMPLES OF METAPHORS

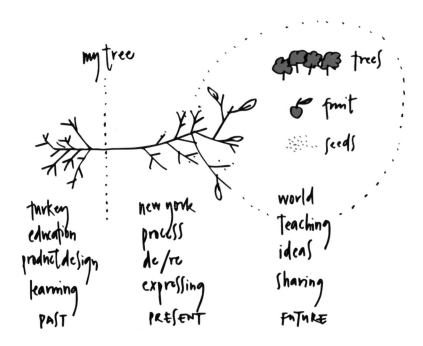

my tree

trees

fruit

seeds

turkey	new york	world
education	process	Teaching
product design	de/re	ideas
learning	expressing	sharing
PAST	PRESENT	FUTURE

My life is a tree

Its roots are in Turkey, its growth in New York, and its fruit
will be all over. A friend asked me "what kind of tree?" and
I defined it as a pomegranate tree—bountiful, beautiful, and
in an orchard of my own making.

Ayse Birsel

My life is Cirque du Soleil

"Colorful, playful, creative, energetic, humanitarian, global, choreographed, chaotic, breathtaking, universal, limit-breaking, epic, collaborative, daring, original, multi-locational, passionate, exceeding the impossible, dynamic, rooted, and in motion."

Marian Gibbon, strategic advisor

My life is a flying machine

A fellow mom with her share of responsibilities described her
life tomorrow as a flying machine: bursts of intense freedom,
lightness, and ability to see things from a bird's-eye view,
with long periods on earth in between flights taking care
of the ground crew, her family.

Nadine Frenette, VP at real-estate firm and mother

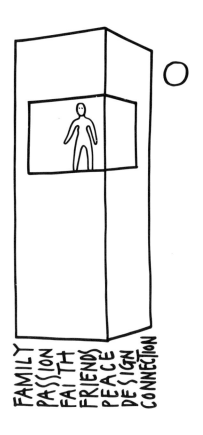

My Life is a glass elevator

"My life is a freestanding glass elevator, firmly secured on a foundation built with family, passion, faith, friendship, peace, design, and connection. There are no limits to how high this elevator can go, but every new level requires a new awareness and appreciation of what is around me, as well as of my role."

Lola Adele-Oso, designer, change accelerator, and community activist

YOUR METAPHORS
Tool #5

Pick a metaphor for today. And then one for the future.

Write about your metaphor and draw it. Or draw it first and then write about what you drew. The more detail the better, as these will provide you with hooks to help you define your life.

Don't overthink it. Remember, we're thinking by doing. You can always change your metaphor. Revisit page 117 for idea starters. And if that is not enough, google "life metaphors" and see!

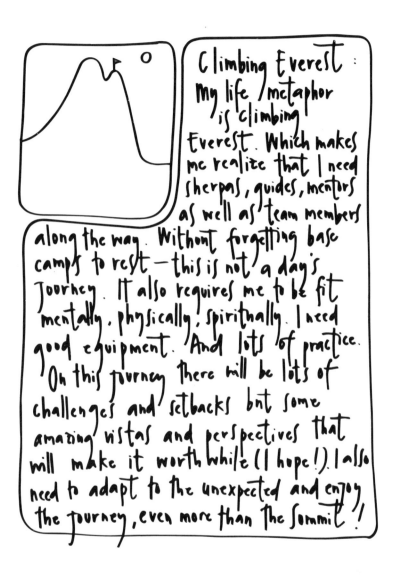

Climbing Everest :
My life /metaphor
is climbing
Everest. Which makes
me realize that I need
sherpas, guides, mentors
as well as team members
along the way. Without forgetting base
camps to rest — this is not a day's
Journey. It also requires me to be fit
mentally, physically, spiritually. I need
good equipment. And lots of practice.
On this journey there will be lots of
challenges and setbacks but some
amazing vistas and perspectives that
will make it worthwhile (I hope!). I also
need to adapt to the unexpected and enjoy
the journey, even more than the summit!

Here is life as climbing Mount Everest. The choice of Everest informs us of
a very specific life design, one that aims at a pinnacle very few people can
or will reach. I call it my CEO metaphor! Note that the more specific you
can make your metaphor, the stronger the insights it will lead you to will be.

TODAY

Using a metaphor, describe your life today, the way it is,
and draw it.

⏱ Timing: 10 minutes

My life today is   ....

....

....

....

....

....

Draw your metaphor for your life today here!

TOMORROW

Now let's shift from today to the future. Using a metaphor, describe your life tomorrow and draw it.

🕐 Timing: 10 minutes

My life tomorrow will be ....

....

....

....

....

....

If you get stuck writing about your metaphor, do the drawing. And then go back to add new details to your writing. You'll be surprised how one can help the other.

Draw your metaphor for your life tomorrow here!

REFLECTION TIME

Look at your metaphors side by side... how will you get from here (today) to there (tomorrow)?

Say your life today is a hike up the mountains and you want to climb up Mt. Everest tomorrow. How will you get from a hike to climbing the highest mountain in the world? You would train differently, get the right gear, find the best Sherpas. And in your life you would get executive training, the right time management tools, and a great mentor.

Write down the first steps you'd need to take
to get started:

The first thing I would do is...

1. ....

2. ....

3. ....

4. ....

5. ....

6. ....

7. ....

8. ....

BEFORE YOU RECONSTRUCT, LET'S TAKE STOCK...

I want you to take a moment to look back at all of the work that you've done and gather the important pieces to select your "key ingredients."

What are the things that really matter to you? Go back and look through your book and highlight or put stars next to things that are dear to your heart, that rise to the top, and that you want to hold on to. You want to make sure to include them in your life.

Make a list of about 15 to 20 words of things that matter.

Here is my list. Take 5 minutes to make yours on the next pages.

Finding beauty

Loving

Being loved

Freedom

Being a good mom

Being a good wife

Showing up

Being original

Being true to self

Honesty

Learning

New experiments

Key ingredients for the life I love:

These are words generated at a workshop I did in Tokyo!

adventure   contributing
closeness   feeling happy
stability   fulfillment
creativity   originality
innovation   sustainability
sense of being   new encounters
rewarded
time w/friends   loving/being loved
excitement   space
fun   comfort
something delicious being flexible
finding beauty   sense of security
freedom   growth
attractive men   wealth
peace   attraction
being useful   diversity

Use these word lists, as well as your work up until this page, as your
word bank.

These are from a workshop I did in New York!

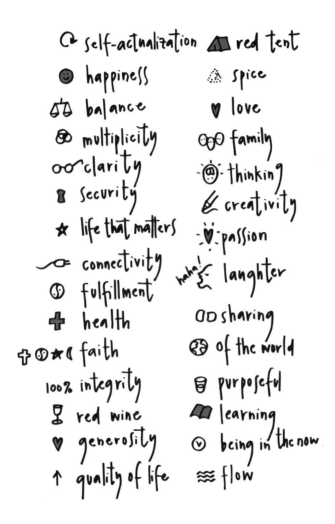

- self-actualization
- happiness
- balance
- multiplicity
- clarity
- security
- life that matters
- connectivity
- fulfillment
- health
- faith
- 100% integrity
- red wine
- generosity
- quality of life

- red tent
- spice
- love
- family
- thinking
- creativity
- passion
- laughter
- sharing
- of the world
- purposeful
- learning
- being in the now
- flow

Self-actualization, the first word, gives away that this is a New York list, at least in my mind.

= unique

Reconstruction
＊

03. RECONSTRUCTION

"Look closely at the present you are constructing: it should look like the future you are dreaming."

You too looked at your present closely, using Deconstruction and POV, your first two steps. Your third step, Reconstruction, builds solidly on them to project you into the future.

ALICE WALKER

RECONSTRUCTION
STEP #3

Reconstruction, our third step, is about putting it back together. It is the other side of Deconstruction.

Let's think back to our soup example for a second. Remember choosing tofu over chicken, freezing it, and putting it on a stick? These choices led us to design a soup pop, a brand-new space soup.

Now you get to choose what you want in your life—what to keep, what to leave out, and what to change. Your choices will determine the kind of life you are designing.

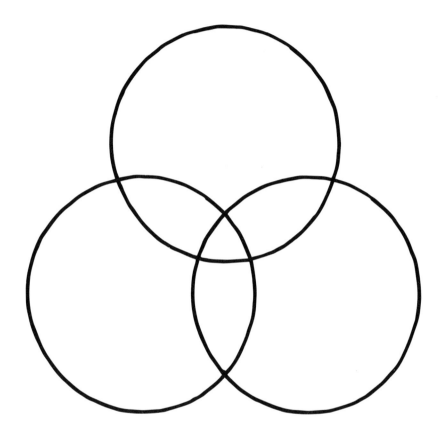

Reconstruction is about making choices. And, let's be frank, you can't have everything. That is why your Reconstruction Map has only three circles representing a small, manageable number of choices. What you choose to put in these circles becomes the backbone of your design.

IN MY WORK RECONSTRUCTION LOOKS LIKE THIS

One of my favorite reconstructions was for Teneo, which I also discussed on pages 32-33. We decided that our three key ingredients were:

1. Structure

2. Utility

3. Cladding

This reconstruction became the foundation for a brand-new way of making storage, one that has 20 parts with which you could create almost an infinite number of combinations. We stopped at 80!

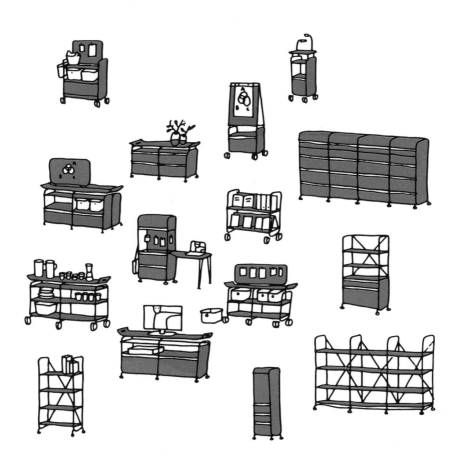

LET'S RECONSTRUCT
Tool #6 ⊂⊃

Let's reconstruct your life!

This is a good time to leaf through your book and revisit your insights, values, metaphors, and key ingredients. What do they tell you about the choices you need to make for the life you love?

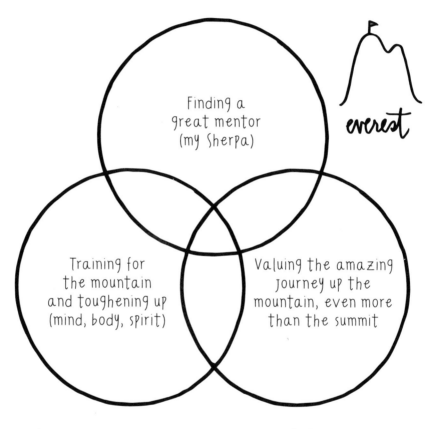

Finding a
great mentor
(my Sherpa)

everest

Training for
the mountain
and toughening up
(mind, body, spirit)

Valuing the amazing
journey up the
mountain, even more
than the summit

AVOID: Complacency!

Note how the Reconstruction Map distills the Everest metaphor into a handful of choices. It sharpens your thinking and focuses your attention on what matters.

Nadine Frenette's Reconstruction, based on her metaphor, the Personal Flying Machine:

flying machine

Freedom to choose
my own direction

Taking care
of the ground
crew

Financially
independent to
be able to fuel
my own Plane

AVOID: Getting Bogged Down

Remember that Nadine is a great mom and so even though her moments of freedom are really key to the life she loves, so is the need to make sure that the ground crew (her family!) is well taken care of.

Carla Diana's Reconstruction based on her Design Studio:

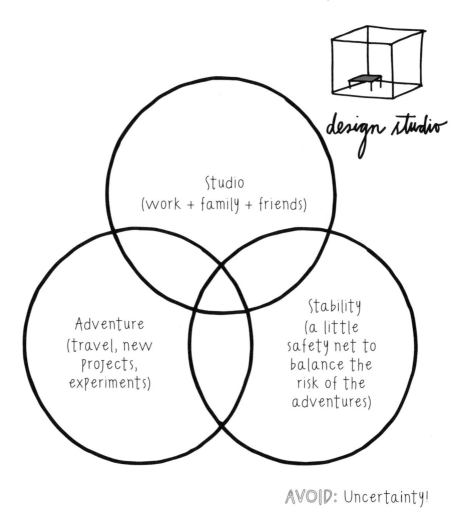

design studio

Studio
(work + family + friends)

Adventure
(travel, new
projects,
experiments)

Stability
(a little
safety net to
balance the
risk of the
adventures)

AVOID: Uncertainty!

Carla Diana's reconstruction map holds her design studio, her wonderful
sense of adventure and, just in case, a little safety net to fall back on.

NOW IT'S YOUR TURN

Pick the three things you absolutely want to have in your life. Note what you are leaving out or want to avoid.

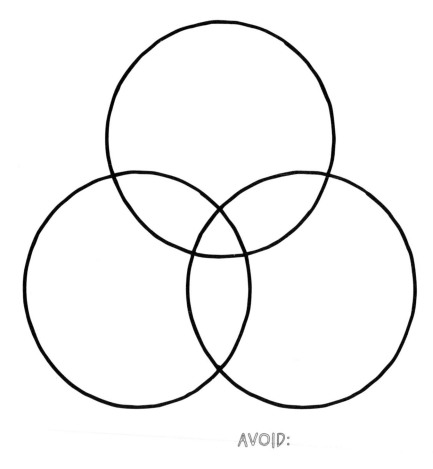

AVOID:

Timing: 5 minutes

Here is another map if you would like to play some more!

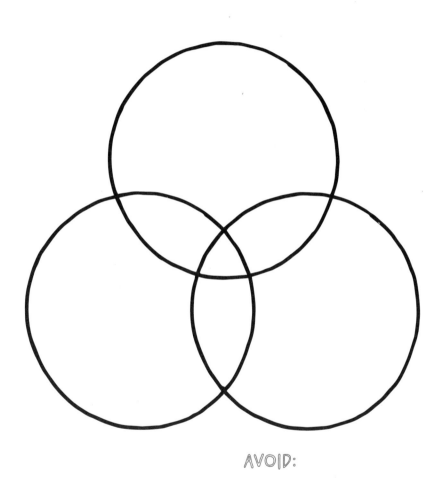

AVOID:

RE:FOUR QUADRANTS
Tool #7

Remember how you deconstructed your life across the four quadrants on page 80? Let's now reconstruct your life in the same way.

Choose the key emotional, physical, intellectual and spiritual elements you absolutely want to have in the life you love. You can refer to your ingredients lists on page 140-141 for reminders.

⏱ Timing: 2.5 minutes per quadrant, 10 minutes total. Reconstruction should be quick. Go with your gut feeling!

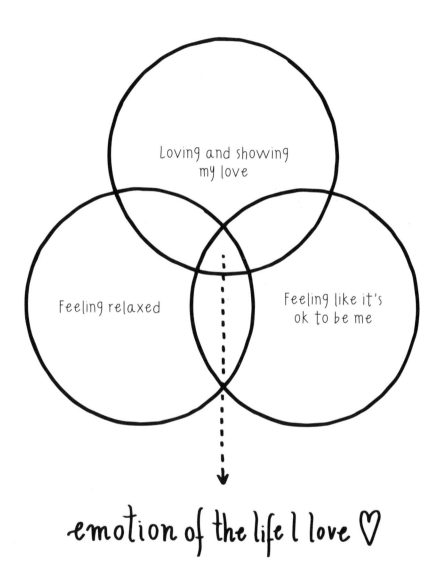

Loving and showing
my love

Feeling relaxed

Feeling like it's
ok to be me

emotion of the life I love ♡

Look at your choices. Say the words. Do they make you happy? Do they capture your imagination? In other words, do they belong in your life? If they do, then include them.

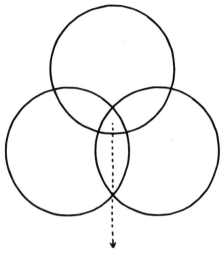

emotion of the life I love ♡

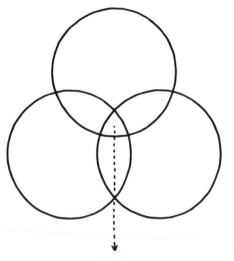

intellect of the life I love @

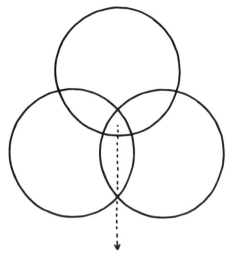

physical of the life I love 🤚

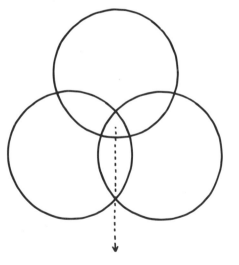

spirit of the life I love Ⓢ

 = unique

Expression
*

04. EXPRESSION

"Happiness is not something ready made. It comes from your own actions."

I was at a design panel at MoMA a few years ago where the moderator, my friend Jamer Hunt, asked me, "Ayse, what if the life someone designs doesn't lead to happiness? What do you do then?" Turn the page for the answer!

DALAI LAMA

EXPRESSION
Step #4

Design is thinking by doing. You have been thinking by doing the exercises that provide you with information about your present life and your vision for the life you love. By weaving them together you can create multiple life expressions before you choose one to "prototype" and live.

Your expression is the voice of who you are and the life you want to live.

To answer Jamer's question from page 164, designing your life is not about happiness, but rather about creating an original life, one that looks and feels like you.

one + one = unique

The sum of all the steps leads to expression, but a great expression is more than the sum of its parts. Expression of the life you love defines who you are and the life you want to live. It is the pursuit of a life well lived.

EXPRESSION IS THE ART OF GIVING FORM TO AN IDEA

You can express your ideas through words, letters, poems, manifestos, and books; sketches, drawings, images, and films; songs, music, and dance; models, prototypes, products, and experiences.

Expression helps you communicate with yourself: to remind, to reinforce, and to refine.

Expression also helps you communicate with others: to share, to convince, and to lead.

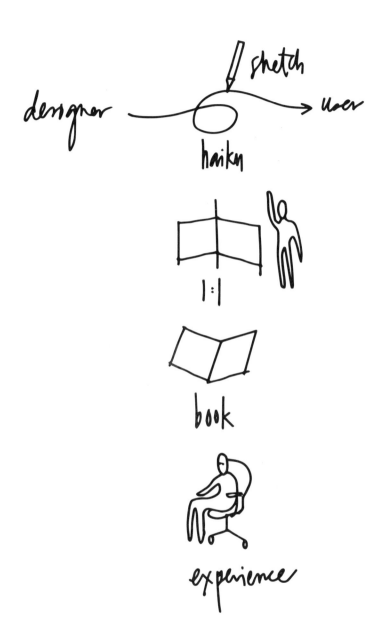

There are so many beautiful ways to express a design!

CREATING YOUR EXPRESSIONS

Here are a few different ways to express the life you want
to live... start with the ones that are easy for you but
also push yourself with those you're less comfortable with...
If you're a writer, try to also draw it; if you are a designer,
do the writing, etc...

Most important, have fun and play!

A NEW MODEL FOR INNOVATION FOR DESIGN + BUSINESS THINKERS

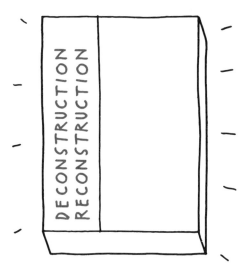

BY AYSE BIRSEL
PUBLISHED BY LARS MULLER
DE/RE © 2011
PRINTED IN NETHERLANDS

FORWORD BY ___ PAOLA, RALPH, CORDY JULIE
BLURBS BY MARSHALL GOLDSMITH,
STEVE JOBS, JOHN MAEDA ...

This was my first expression for this book that you're holding in your hands.
I drew it on a large easel Post-it to put a stake in the ground and to share
it with my family. Note that this was some years ago, and the book evolved
into what it is today, but this was the starting point.

VISION MAP AS EXPRESSION

Create a vision map of the Life You Love.

Draw yourself at the center.

Add visual details that relate to your life. Use pull quotes to add as much detail to your vision as you can.

Turn the page for a template.

⏱ Timing: 10 minutes.

MY GOAL IS TO BE THE KATY PERRY of
DESIGN THE LIFE YOU LOVE ♡ AYSE BIRSEL

USA EU JAPAN ⛳ THE TOUR ⛳ 2016

FRIENDS   FAMILY

design the life you love

LEAH
the guide

SEDA
the closer

BIBI the force

AWA+ALEV+WALY
the future

ISSEY
MIYAKE
the costumes!

MURAT
the brother

JZ:
the scaler

FOLLOWERS

TISH
the gamer

HIROKO
SAKOMURA
the producer

NOREEN
MORIOKA
+NICOLE
the communicators

BROWN
the educator

EXEC TOUR PRODUCER
TBD

PR

WRITER

♡TOUR BOOK APP GAME EDUCATION SOCIAL NETWORK 🐦

Here is my vision map from 2014: to be the Katy Perry of Design the Life You
Love, inspired by *Part of Me*, the film about her tour. It made me think about
taking a design show on the road with my family and friends, and connecting
with young audiences about design at a very accessible level.

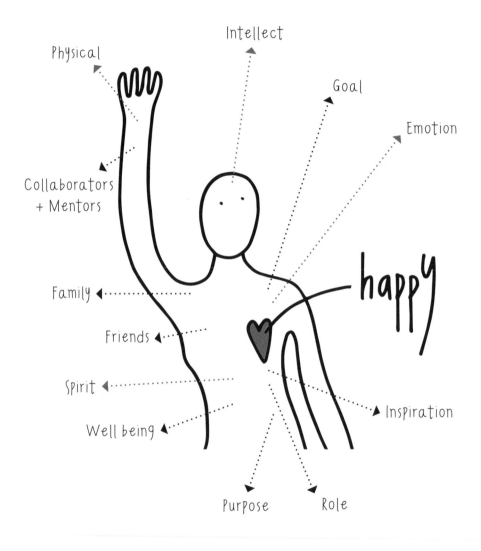

Physical

Intellect

Goal

Emotion

Collaborators
+ Mentors

happy

Family

Friends

Spirit

Inspiration

Well being

Purpose

Role

Here are some suggestions for completing the next page. It is like a recap of everything you've done so far.

The Life I Love

happy

Add your glasses, tools of your trade, your environment, and little details that make this yours.

Draw your own vision map here!

Draw your own vision map here!

Note: Once completed, display your map prominently at home. You can redraw it poster size and hang it in the bedroom like I did. It will generate conversations to help you share your design with your family.

VISION LETTER AS EXPRESSION

Write a letter to yourself about The Life You Love.

Use your vision map as a template to flesh out your thoughts as fully as possible.

Submit your letter using the form on: www.futureme.org and choose a return date for when you want to receive it.

Here are some pointers to help you flesh out your vision letter, using everything you've done so far in this book.

⏱ Timing: 10-15 minutes.

Month / date / year

Dear ___ (person you're addressing your letter to: yourself, partner, husband, wife, daughter/son)

I deconstructed my life recently and realized ___(your insights, constraints, opportunities here). My heroes are ___ (your heroes here) and they remind me of my own values ___ (your values here). Actually, my life today is a ___ and I am redesigning it to be ___ in the future (add your metaphors with enough detail to talk about your life today vs. your life vision here). This led me to reconstruct my life to include what really matters to me (your choices across emotional, physical, intellectual, and spiritual here). This is the life I love, and I wanted to share it with you. ___ (conclusion, next steps, why this was important to you here).

Your Name

.... (date)   your letter here

....

....

....

....

....

....

....

....

....

....

....

....

....

....

....

....

....

....

.... (signature)

.... (date)   your letter here

....

....

....

....

....

....

....

....

....

....

....

....

....

....

....

....

.... (signature)

183

TO-DO LIST AS EXPRESSION

Make a to-do list for the Life You Love.

Fill in your to-do's. Look at "how to get from here to there" from your metaphors. Tape your list to your desk. Check the boxes when done.

Turn the page for a template.

⏱ Timing: 10 minutes.

MEGAN'S TO-DO'S:

GREAT-FUN-BIG-OLE' TO DO's!

1) HAVE OR RAISE KIDS
2) BUILD A HAPPY PLACE TO WORK
3) STEVE'S CORONA POSTER
4) GROW A POMEGRANATE TREE
5) HOST A BIG WONDERFUL THANKSGIVING
6) BUILD HAPPY RITUALS
7) VISIT MORE W/ MY MOM
8) KEEP ON SKATING!
9) MAKE JEWELRY

Megan Neese is a designer, futurist, and a natural designer of life. She made this list in 10 minutes at my workshop. I like how she mixes up the big and small to-do's. Last I checked, she had planted a pomegranate tree in her friend's yard.

TO-DO'S FOR THE LIFE I LOVE

✓

☐ _____ .

☐ _____ .

☐ _____ .

☐ _____ .

☐ _____ .

☐ _____ .

☐ _____ .

☐ _____ .

Don't forget to include long- + short-term,
as well as serious + playful to-do's!

TO-DO'S FOR THE LIFE I LOVE

✓

☐ _____.

☐ _____.

☐ _____.

☐ _____.

☐ _____.

☐ _____.

☐ _____.

☐ _____.

MANIFESTO AS EXPRESSION

Write a manifesto for your life.

Your manifesto is your public declaration of your opinions and goals. A great example is Bruce Mau's "An Incomplete Manifesto For Growth" (www.manifestoproject.it/bruce-mau).

Turn the page for a template. Make one- or two-sentence declarations.

⏱ Timing: 10-15 minutes.

1. ENJOY THE SIMPLE THINGS! making my bed, washing dishes, reading to the kids, cooking.

2. HAVE CREATIVE HABITS! à la Twyla Twarp. continue to wake up early, sketch every day.

3. BE CREATIVE W/ THE KIDS! make stuff. figure out new ways to engage them. give funny answers + ask questions.

4. ALWAYS EXPERIMENT! try new things, plan carefully, do dry runs w/ friends. then do it.

5. DO THINGS FOR YOURSELF! Just like your mom always told you. see Rome. play tennis! karate

6. DROP WHATEVER DOESN'T BRING JOY! worrying, nostalgia, wishing it wasn't so... envy...

This is my manifesto for the life I love. I feel like there can be more things to add to this list, so I am still working on it. It is unfinished, like Bruce Mau's.

MY LIFE'S MANIFESTO

State a belief, an action, or an intention. Explain it with a few sentences. This is your call to action.

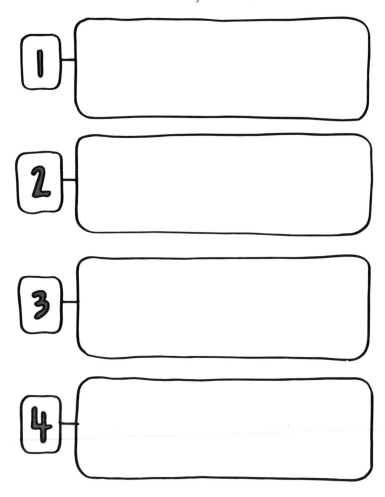

1

2

3

4

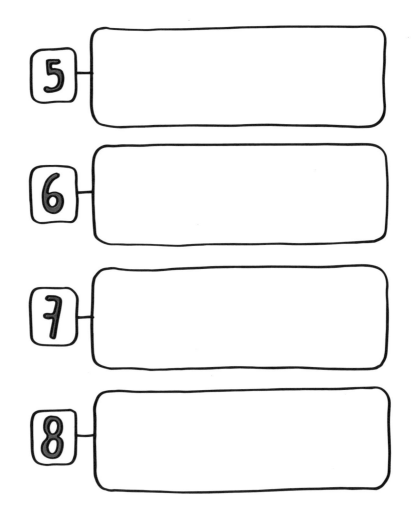

5

6

7

8

MY LIFE'S MANIFESTO

Continue if yours is unfinished (like mine) and add to it over time.

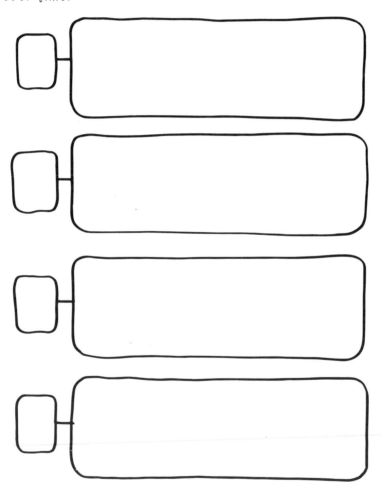

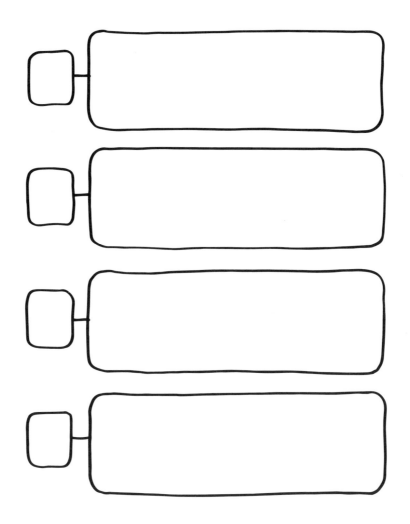

POEM AS EXPRESSION

Write a poem about The Life You Love.

For some of us a poem is a powerful way of capturing our stream of consciousness. If you're one of them, like Janet Parks who wrote Growth Is Now, this is for you.

Turn the page for a template.

⏱ Timing: 10-15 minutes.

GROWTH IS NOW

I am drought tolerant, disease resistant, I persevere
My large branches unfold
Nests, each year, chirp with change and excitement
Broad branches offer shade when it's too hot for others
~my growth will come

When rain falls, I smile and pull the water near,
holding the precious moisture close
~my growth will come

Always busy, always social, everyone gathers near
my roots
Feeling refreshed when they leave
~my growth will come

Buds appear, drawing in the sun
Fruitful future
~growth is now

Balancing old woods with fresh sprigs
Blossoms daily, fully aware, curtsy at the spring unfolding
~growth is now

We are all powerful
We can solve our own challenges as we advise each
other well

Janet Parks is a retail executive who wrote this beautiful poem. It led her
to new growth: after writing it she redefined what she wanted to do, shared
it with her leadership, and made it happen.

MY LIFE IS A POEM

Write a poem to express your life design à la Janet Parks.

....

....

....

....

....

....

....

MY LIFE IS A HAIKU

Write a haiku to express your life design in the 3 line, 17 syllable, 5-7-5 structure in the Japanese style, or the 12 syllables and a 3-5-3 syllable "free form" more suited to English. Or simply 3 lines, "my form"!

....

....

....

Here is a haiku written for me from @TheHaikuGuys:

materials sourced
every day master-crafter
layers on layers

#freehaiku

 = unique

LIVING THE LIFE

NELSON MANDELA

"It always seems
impossible until
it's done."

Who better than Nelson Mandela, master designer of life and hero,
to remind us that we will never know if we don't try.

Portrait by Bibi Seck.

LET'S RETRACE OUR STEPS...

00.
INTENTION
At one moment in time, you decided, I want to design my life.

01.
DECON-STRUCTION
The way to design anything new is to break our preconceptions. That was our starting point.

02.
POINT OF VIEW
You can make happen what you visualize. This is what we did using heroes and metaphors.

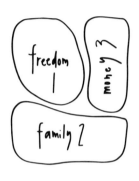

03.
RECON-
STRUCTION
Deconstruction
without
Reconstruction is
incomplete. We
tried different
permutations
until we decided
what really
matters.

04.
EXPRESSION
Every design is an
expression of an
intention. Here is
where we gave
form to our design
through words,
drawings, poems,
to-do lists.

05.
LIVING
There is only
one way to test
a new design:
by trying it out.
Which brings us
to our last step.
Go, live the life
you love.

LIVING THE LIFE!

The next step is to live the life you love!

Here are a couple of design steps you can take to get started.
They include modeling, learning, sharing, visualizing,
and prototyping.

MODELING

Look at your Reconstruction Maps (pages 156-161). What are places where you're already doing this in your life?

Can you find examples where they already exist and then model those experiences to have more of them in your life?

You can also look to others for inspiration—your heroes, mentors, friends, teachers, books—and see if you can model solutions from them to your own design.

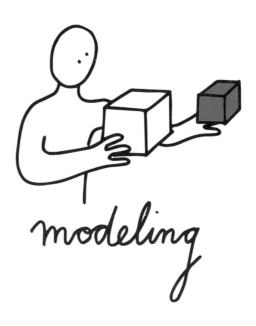

modeling

LEARNING

New designs often mean new skills.

Think about where and how you can learn these new skills.

You can learn by going to school, taking online courses, finding a mentor, tag teaming with a friend to learn from each other, and reading books.

Don't forget to practice. Create opportunities to practice what you learned (see Prototyping, page 209).

learning

SHARING

Designers are good collaborators, as design is often a collaborative effort. You will probably need support to realize your design.

Share your design expression with others and enlist their help. Listen to their feedback. Learn from their expertise.

And when in doubt about who to listen to, refer back to your values (pages 110-111) and Reconstruction Maps (pages 156-161) to remind yourself of your design intentions.

sharing

VISUALIZING

Designers are good visualizers. If you can visualize your ideal life or self, you can work toward realizing it.

Place your Vision Map (page 175) on your desk or on your wall—someplace where you can refer to it easily. And when you need new designs, continue to use the visualization tools you used in this workbook to generate new maps, posters, and charts to help you visually imagine, sort out, and design new solutions. (See the templates section on page 218, for blank charts.)

visualizing

PROTOTYPING

Prototyping could be living in a city like a local for a couple of weeks before you decide to move there; or taking evening classes before you quit your job and enroll full-time; or moonlighting in something you love to see if you can make a living doing it; or living with your partner to see if you can share a life. It is making a working model as close to reality as possible and testing and refining it, before committing 100 percent.

prototyping

DESIGN THE LIFE
YOU LOVE

Bravo! You've just applied design process and tools to think
about your life differently.

Remember that design is an ongoing process and one you
get better at with practice.

But the best way to learn it is to teach the process
to someone else. Help others design their lives!

warm-up

deconstruct

inspiration

today

tomorrow

choice

goals

design

living

Remember the steps of the process. Use them when you're trying to make decisions. Deconstruct a problem. Gather inspiration from your heroes. Imagine a solution using a metaphor. Reconstruct to explore your choices. Express them by drawing or writing. Test them out.

THE PURPOSE...

The point of Design the Life You Love is to have an original life that is coherent with who you are—a life that feels like you, that looks like you, that is you. It is using design process to think differently about life; imagining positive possibilities within given constraints; taking risks; asking "what if" questions to think anew; prototyping, testing and tinkering, and prototyping again; and maybe being rewarded for it with a life well lived.

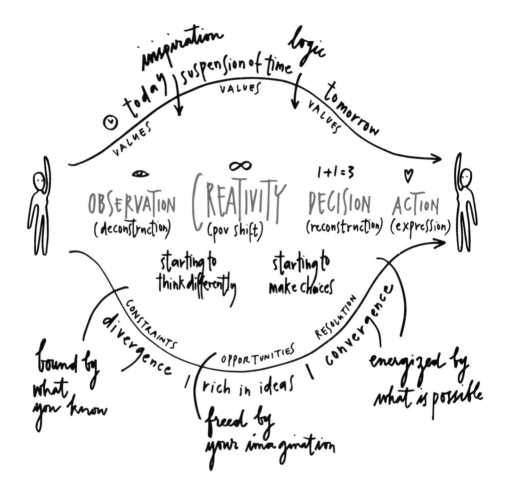

inspiration   logic

today suspension of time tomorrow
VALUES VALUES VALUES VALUES

OBSERVATION CREATIVITY DECISION ACTION
(deconstruction) (pov shift) (reconstruction) (expression)

1+1=3

starting to think differently   starting to make choices

CONSTRAINTS   RESOLUTION
divergence   convergence

bound by what you know

OPPORTUNITIES
rich in ideas

freed by your imagination

energized by what is possible

Design process is one of divergence and convergence. You observe what you deconstructed to think differently about the same things, to create new ideas before you can decide which ideas are strong and worth bringing to life. In the beginning you're bound by what you know, and then you're freed by your imagination and energized by what is possible at the end. Your values are what hold your creative process together.

go ahead and design and

e the life you love!

THE END IS ONLY
THE BEGINNING!

TEMPLATES

This section has blank templates of all the exercises in this book. Now that you've tried them out, use these when you've filled up your book. You can also make photocopies. These will give you a chance to practice.

Once you've gotten the hang of it, you can draw them in your own sketchbook, freestyle.

Let the rabbit remind you to continue being playful! This one is Bibi's.
You can draw your own rabbit or make your own "playful" symbol.

Warm Up: Draw Someone

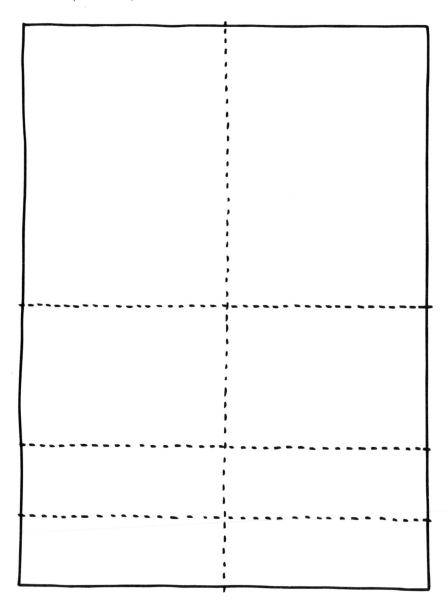

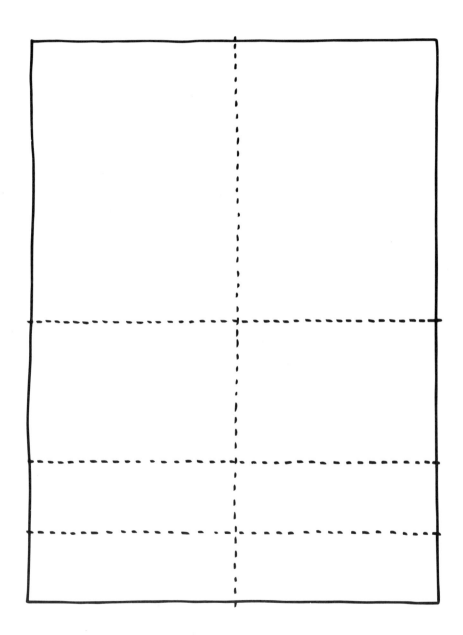

Let's deconstruct! Feel free to spill onto the next page.

Deconstruction:
Four Quadrants

- -

Deconstruction Recap

insights AHA!

too little/too much 🧪

opportunity +

constraints —

Your Heroes

my hero: _____
_____
_____
_____
_____

□

icon/symbol

my hero: _____
_____
_____
_____
_____

□

icon/symbol

my hero: _____
_____
_____
_____
_____

icon/symbol

my hero: _____
_____
_____
_____
_____

icon/symbol

Your Metaphor for Today

My life today is ....

....

....

....

....

....

....

drawing

231

Your Metaphor for the Future

My life tomorrow will be ....

....

....

....

....

....

....

drawing

233

Key Ingredients for the Life You Love

235

Let's reconstruct!

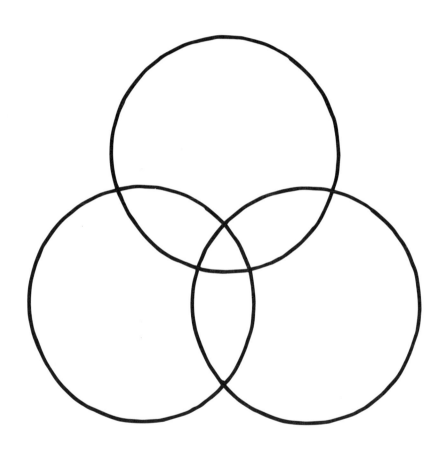

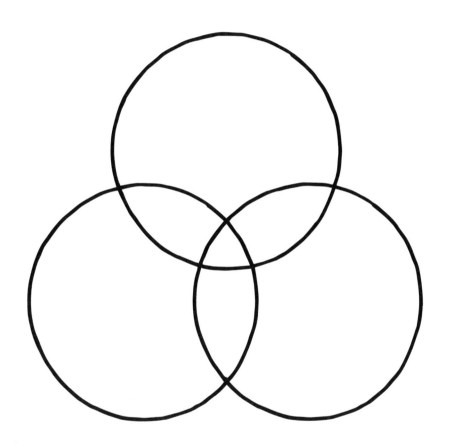

237

Reconstruction:
Four Quadrants

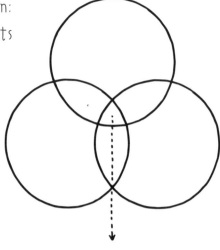

emotion of the life I love ♡

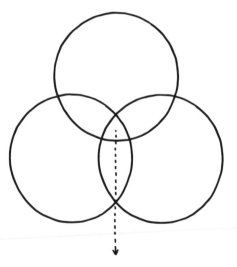

intellect of the life I love ☺

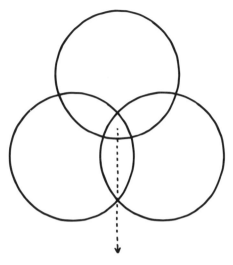

physical of the life I love

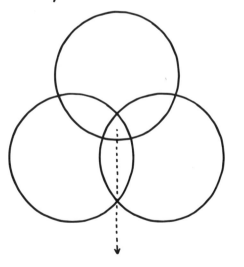

spirit of the life I love

239

Vision Map as Expression

happy

Draw Your Own Vision Map

Vision Letter as Expression

(date) ....

....

....

....

....

....

....

....

....

....

....

....

....

....

....

....

....

.... (signature)

To-Do List as Expression

✓

☐ _____ .

☐ _____ .

☐ _____ .

☐ _____ .

☐ _____ .

☐ _____ .

☐ _____ .

☐ _____ .

✓

☐ _____ .

☐ _____ .

☐ _____ .

☐ _____ .

☐ _____ .

☐ _____ .

☐ _____ .

☐ _____ .

Manifesto as Expression

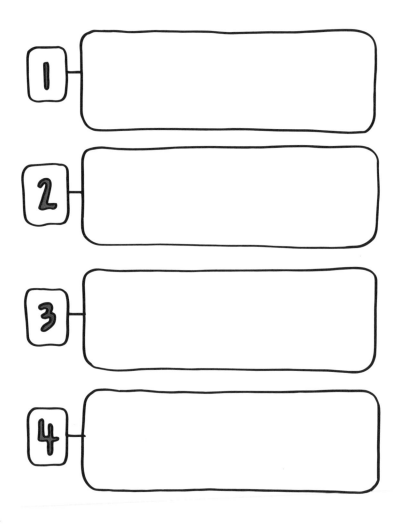

1

2

3

4

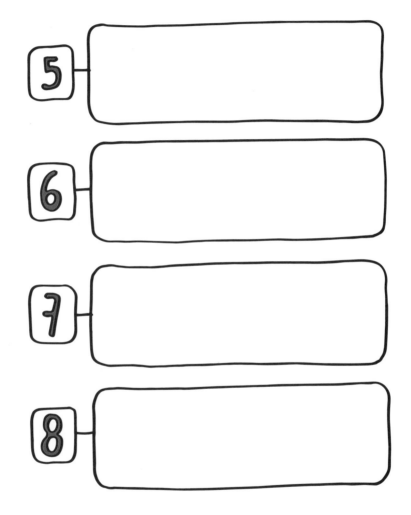

5

6

7

8

Poem as Expression

....

....

....

....

....

....

....

....

Haiku as Expression

....

....

....

....

....

....

READING LIST

This is a list of books I read while writing this book that I found inspirational.

- *By Design: Why There Are No Locks on the Bathroom Doors in the Hotel Louis XIV and Other Object Lessons* by Ralph Caplan

- *The Happiness Hypothesis: Finding Modern Truth in Ancient Wisdom* by Jonathan Haidt

- *The 4-Hour Workweek* by Timothy Ferriss

- *NLP at Work: The Essence of Excellence* by Sue Knight

- Bruce Mau's Incomplete Manifesto for Growth www.manifestoproject.it/bruce-mau/

- *The Creative Habit: Learn It And Use It For Life* by Twyla Tharp

- *How Proust Can Change Your Life* by Alain de Botton

- *Spark: How Creativity Works* by Julie Burstein

- *The Art of Possibility* by Rosamund Stone Zander and Benjamin Zander

- *The Social Animal* by David Brooks

- *Manage Your Day-To-Day: Build Your Routine, Find Your Focus & Sharpen Your Creative Mind* edited by Jocelyn Glei

- *The Life-Changing Magic of Tidying Up* by Marie Kondo

ABOUT THE AUTHOR

Ayse Birsel has been designing award-winning products for over 2o years. She is the co-founder of Birsel + Seck, an innovative design studio in New York that partners with leading brands and Fortune 5oo companies including GE, Herman Miller, Hewlett Packard, Johnson & Johnson, Nissan, Target, Toyota, and TOTO, among others. Ayse is also known for her acclaimed workshops, Design the Life You Love, the foundation of this book. She lives between New York and Istanbul with her husband and partner Bibi Seck and their three kids, who continue to inspire her life design.

Design the Life You Love transformed my thinking. I used to be a designer of things, but now I am a designer of life.

thank you*!

This book wouldn't have been possible without the help, support, generous spirit, and inspiration of some very special people.

Thank you my beloved family-starting with my parents, Ozgul and Mahmut Birsel; Murat Birsel; Alev Bilgen; Gisele and Mamadou Seck; and Bibi Seck, my life partner, and our children, Awa, Alev and Waly, all beautiful co-designers of my life.

Thank you my brilliant team, all of whom are also my dear friends-Leah Caplan, who held my hand every step of the way; Seda Evis, who held the ship together while we worked on the book; Rona Binay, who designed the first draft; and Lee Iley, who loaned his discerning eye.

Thank you my dear friends and champions-Shirley Moulton, Ralph Caplan, Keith Yamashita, Stefan Sagmeister, Jocelyne Beaudoin, David Carroll, Anni Kuan, Marshall Goldsmith, Clark Malcolm, Alice Twemlow, Emily Weiner, Allan Chochinov, Steven Heller, Hiroko Sakomura, John Zapolski, Kellie Kulton, Yilmaz Aysan, Ela Cindoruk, and Jocelyn Glei, my fairy godmother.

Thank you my dear teachers, Rowena Reed Kostellow and Bruce Hannah, who taught me to have confidence.

Thank you dear participants of my workshops-everyone who came and taught me so much, especially Carla Diana, Hani Hong, Michael Robinson, Marion Gibbon, Nadine Frenette, Lolo Adele-Oso, Megan Neese, and Janet Parks, who were generous enough to allow me to use their designs in this book.

Thank you my dear agent, Meg Thompson, without whom this book wouldn't have seen the light of day.

Thank you dear Ten Speed Press team-Aaron Wehner, Hannah Rahill, Emma Campion, Julie Bennett, Michele Crim, and Virginia Rhoda. Thanks most of all to my wonderful publicist Daniel Wikey, to masterful Kara Plikaitis, who designed the book and, last but not least, to my dear editor Kaitlin Ketchum, who guided me so beautifully through the process.

And to the muse of design and drawing who sometimes made it flow and sometimes withheld the love, I know you were there all along, especially when everyone else was asleep. Thank you.

Published in the United States by Ten Speed Press,
an imprint of the Crown Publishing Group, a division
of Penguin Random House LLC, New York.
www.crownpublishing.com
www.tenspeed.com

Ten Speed Press and the Ten Speed Press colophon are
registered trademarks of Penguin Random House LLC.

Birsel, Ayse.
Design the life you love : a guide to thinking about your
life playfully and with optimism / Ayse Birsel.
pages cm
Includes bibliographical references and index.
1. Creative ability. 2. Self-actualization (Psychology)
3. Motivation (Psychology) I. Title.
BF408.B487 2015
158.1–dc23
2015014360

Trade Paperback ISBN: 978-1-60774-881-6
eBook ISBN: 978-1-60774-882-3

Printed in China

Design by Kara Plikaitis

10 9 8 7 6 5 4 3 2 1

First Edition